Everything a child needs to know about ADHD

For children aged 6 to 12 years

By Dr C R Yemula

ADDiS
ADHD INFORMATION SERVICES
Registered Charity No: 1070827

D1437652

To my children Nikitha and Nehal

2nd Edition printed November 2007
First published in the UK in 2006 by ADDISS
The National Attention Deficit Disorder Information and Support Service
Registered Charity No 1070827
2nd floor, Premier House
112 Station Road
Edgware
HA8 7BJ
Email: info@addiss.co.uk
www.addiss.co.uk

ISBN 978-0-9554033-3-0

Please note:
The information presented in this book is intended as a
support to professional advice and care. It is not a
substitute for a medical diagnosis or treatment.

Contents

Dear Parents/Carers

Coming to terms with the diagnosis of ADHD is not always easy and most parents wonder how they are going to explain the condition to their children. Dr Yemula has taken a lot of care to make that journey easier for you.

This book aims to explain some of the important aspects of ADHD, in the format of a simple story and colourful illustrations, for children aged between 6 and 12 years. It may be helpful for both you and your child to read it together, in stages.

ADHD has a significant impact on a child's overall function with a knock-on effect for learning, behaviour and family and social relationships. Children with ADHD need early identification and intervention with appropriate medical and/or behavioural and educational support, in order to maximise their potential and safeguard their mental health.

Helping your child with ADHD, to better understand and take ownership of the condition will ensure they are more likely to comply with a management plan, which in turn will improve their quality of life.

With best wishes

Andrea Bilbow
Chief Executive
ADDISS

Dear Reader

This book is about Tom and Laura who both have ADHD, which is a medical condition. There are many children like Tom and Laura who are having problems at home and at school.

Don't feel bad if you have ADHD.
It is not your fault! Nobody is perfect.
For example, some children have Diabetes and some have Asthma.

This book will give you general information about ADHD. Both Tom and Laura had lots of problems. However, you may not have all the difficulties they had.

Tom worked very hard to get better.
Laura was also successful.

Like Tom and Laura, you too can do well.

Dr C R Yemula

Here is the story of Tom which will tell you a lot more about ADHD.

Tom is a 6 year old boy who lives with his family in a small village. He has a little sister called Jenny who is 3 years old.

Tom's dad works at a motor company and has to travel to the city everyday.

Tom goes to the local school. His mum stays at home to look after Jenny.

Tom likes lots of sports and his favourite one is football. Tom and his family are keen supporters of the local football team.

Champions United

One day mum and dad took Tom to see a specialist doctor, as he was having some problems both at home and school.

The doctor asked some questions to find out what was happening at Tom's school and at home.

The doctor took detailed notes about Tom's birth and development.

He then looked at all the reports and information sent to him by Tom's parents and the school. Tom's school report had lots of details about his attention, behaviour and learning ability.

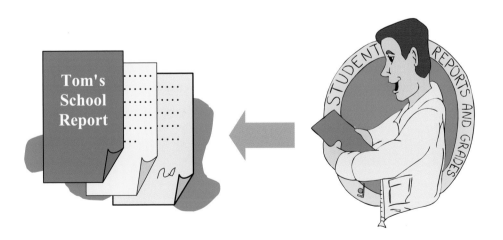

The teacher says Tom is restless, fidgety and does not sit still for more than a few minutes in class.

Mrs Wright

Tom finds it hard to concentrate and tends to distract other children. He is very chatty, butts into games and interrupts others while they are talking.

One day Tom was very noisy in class. He shouted out answers and interrupted the teacher several times during the maths lesson. The teacher told Tom that his behaviour was not acceptable as he was disturbing the whole class.

However, Tom was still loud and noisy and as a result he was sent out of the class. He had to work on his own in the head teacher's office. Tom was sorry about this, but he just could not stay quiet.

Head Teacher

Mr B Strict

The teacher discovered that Tom was getting into trouble in the playground. He was also teased and sometimes bullied.

He is kind and generous to other children. However, he is strong-willed and likes to play on his terms. Sometimes he can be silly and makes faces. As a result he falls out with his friends.

The teacher says that Tom is falling behind in his reading and writing because of his problems.

12
×2
24

Mrs Sharp

Mum says that Tom is always 'on the go' which means he is too active. He tends to rush things and does not finish his homework.

Tom cannot play at anything for very long. He gets bored quickly. He likes to do several things at the same time and can't focus on any single activity.

Sometimes he has temper tantrums if he can't get his own way. He becomes angry, loses his temper and slams doors.

Tom frequently interrupts mum while she is on the telephone. He can be loud and noisy. He can sometimes be very naughty and stubborn. He does not do as he is told.

I love to eat lots of cookies everyday even though mum says I shouldn't

14

Tom is a lovely boy who has good manners. He helps his mum in the kitchen with the washing up and setting the table.

Tom loves his sister Jenny very much. He often helps her to complete jigsaw puzzles. Jenny's favourite toy is the teddy that Tom gave her as a birthday present.

To my lovely sister - Tom

He has a brilliant imagination and enjoys doing creative work.

Tom's drawings

Hello Earthlings!

The nurse checked Tom's weight, height and blood pressure.

The doctor listened to Tom's chest and heart. He then checked Tom's tummy, muscles and nerves and said that Tom was fine. The doctor also did some tests to check Tom's development which were normal.

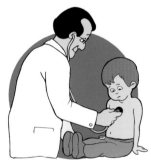

Tom told the doctor that although he liked his school, he was not happy because he did not have many friends.

The doctor explained that Tom has **ADHD**.
There are three kinds of ADHD.

Inattentive

Hyperactive / Impulsive

Combined

Tom has got the Combined type of ADHD because
he has lots of difficulties in the following areas.

Inattention
which means

Poor concentration
Forgetfulness
Poorly organised
Easily distracted

Hyperactivity
which means

Fidgety
Can't sit still
Runs or climbs a lot
Very active, restless

I feel as if there is a motor inside me that goes brrrrrrr all the time

Impulsivity
which means

Very chatty
Not waiting his turn
Interrupting others
Poor sense of danger

Got to say it Got to say it now!!

Tom's Mum and Dad love him very much, although he is sometimes naughty and they don't always like his behaviour.

They were worried when they heard from the doctor that Tom has ADHD. They wanted to know more about ADHD, what it means and how they can help Tom. They asked the doctor lots of questions.

 ⭐ **What is ADHD?** ⭐

ADHD is a medical condition called

'**A**ttention **D**eficit **H**yperactivity **D**isorder'.

Most people call it ADHD because it is easier to say instead of the long name.

Looong Indeed!

Mr Strechy

The doctor said that ADHD is not just another name for naughtiness.

ADHD does not mean naughtiness

All naughtiness is not because of ADHD

A child with ADHD can still be naughty

I shouldn't but I will

Timmy Teazer

Bobby Throball

Some children may be naughty because of their learning difficulties.

Sometimes a child may misbehave at school, if something nasty is going on at home. For example, somebody may be hurting the child.

However, Tom does not have these problems.

Can ADHD make a child less clever?

No. The doctor said that children with ADHD can be as clever as other children of their age. However, they have to work much harder to do well at school.

In a class of 20 to 30 children, one child may have ADHD.

However, out of 100 children only one will have ADHD causing major difficulties.

More boys than girls have ADHD

Although we do not know the exact cause, there are several reasons for having ADHD.

We all have certain chemicals in the brain that help to control our behaviour. A child with ADHD may not have the right balance of these chemicals.

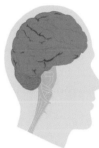

ADHD may be inherited and this means that other family members may also have the condition.

The child is not at fault and ADHD is NOT caused by Bad Parenting or Poor Diet.

Bad Parenting

Poor Diet

The doctor said that sometimes a child with ADHD may have one or other problems such as:

Co-ordination Difficulties
This means bumping into things, spilling drinks and poor handwriting

I wish I could write better

I don't have many friends

Low self - esteem
This means the child feeling not good enough or worthless.

Learning Difficulties
This means problems with reading, writing etc.

Child with ADHD

Poor Social Skills
This means not knowing how to make friends etc.

Oppositional Defiant Behaviour
This means being stubborn, arguing a lot etc.

Conduct Problems
This means telling lies, stealing, setting fire, damaging property etc.

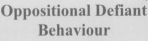

Not necessarily. There is no special test for ADHD.

However, the doctor may ask for blood tests or arrange some special tests to check for other medical conditions.

The doctor said that avoiding fizzy drinks, sweets and colourings in food might help Tom to be less hyperactive and better behaved.

At school Tom can make lots of friends and keep them, by doing certain things.

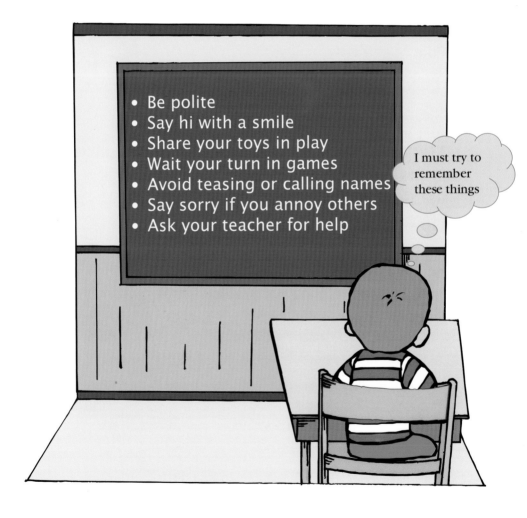

- Be polite
- Say hi with a smile
- Share your toys in play
- Wait your turn in games
- Avoid teasing or calling names
- Say sorry if you annoy others
- Ask your teacher for help

I must try to remember these things

Helpful hints for Tom

The doctor gave Tom a list of things to help with his behaviour.

Ground rules set by mum and dad

- Agree the rules with mum and dad.
- Follow the rules daily.

Make a deal with mum and dad

Write down a list of things you do. Ask mum and dad what they like and improve one thing at a time. For example:

- Do as you are told
- Try not to be too noisy
- Be polite and try not to argue.
- Get dressed in time for school.
- Keep your bedroom nice and tidy.

Reward chart

You can use a Behaviour or Reward chart for doing good things.

- Use stars and stickers.

Helpful hints for Tom

Choose your rewards for doing the right thing

The rewards may be
- 30 minutes extra on the computer
- Watch a video or DVD of your choice.
- 30 minutes extra for football or other games

Try to think first before you say or do something

This will help you to stay out of trouble.
For example:

- Before crossing the road
- While the teacher is talking
- If mum is on the telephone

Wait....
Think....

Get organised and keep a routine

- Make a list of things you need to do every day
- Check your PE kit, books, pencils etc

Mum & Dad can go on a special 'Parent Training Programme'. This would help them to understand Tom's problems and manage his behaviour better.

They now know that Tom is not a problem child but a child who has a medical problem, which is the reason why he misbehaves a lot.

At home Mum & Dad can spend 'quality time' with Tom and also help him to do his homework regularly.

The doctor gave Tom's mum & dad a list of practical hints to help his behaviour.

- Set up a routine at home.
- Give praise and/or rewards when Tom does the right thing.
- Tell Tom straight away if he makes a mistake so that he understands.
- Time out - sometimes Tom may need to be sent to his room or be grounded to help him learn to do the right thing.

The doctor said the teacher can help Tom in many ways.

The teacher knows that Tom has ADHD. However, this should not be an excuse for Tom to misbehave.

The teacher needs to give him small amounts of work, one piece at a time. This will help Tom to concentrate, finish easily and then move on to the next task.

Miss Help Me-lott

It is helpful to cut down on any distractions in class and give Tom plenty of advice when he misbehaves.

Tom can earn points or rewards for good behaviour at school, by following these instructions.

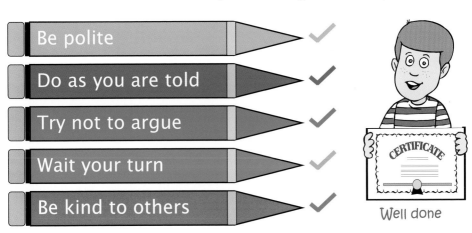

- Be polite
- Do as you are told
- Try not to argue
- Wait your turn
- Be kind to others

Well done

The doctor said that Tom could try a medicine to help him sit still and concentrate better at school. This will in turn, help him to get higher grades and fulfil his potential.

However, medicine is not a quick fix or a cure for ADHD. In addition Tom, his parents and teacher need to follow the behavioural techniques both at home and at school.

Medicine

Helpful Hints
for ....
Tom ....
Parents ....
Teacher ....

Not all children with ADHD need to take medicines. Some can do well with behavioural techniques alone.

The medicines for ADHD come as tablets or capsules and are generally easy to swallow.

The doctor then talked about different medicines, which are given according to what the child needs.

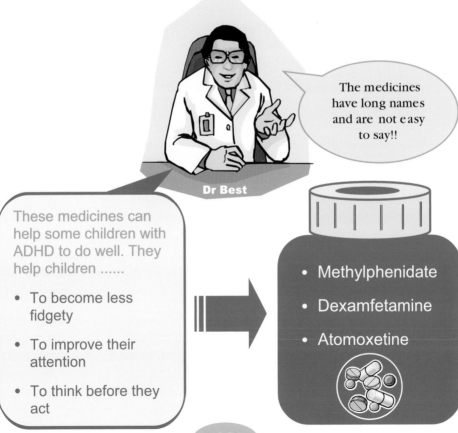

The medicines have long names and are not easy to say!!

Dr Best

These medicines can help some children with ADHD to do well. They help children ......

- To become less fidgety

- To improve their attention

- To think before they act

- Methylphenidate

- Dexamfetamine

- Atomoxetine

33

The medicine Methylphenidate comes in two forms:

 Short - acting medicine

This medicine works for 3-4 hours and is usually taken 2 or 3 times a day at mealtimes. It is called Equasym, Ritalin, Medikinet or just plain Methylphenidate in the UK.

| Breakfast | Lunch | Tea |

 Long - acting medicine

This medicine is taken once a day in the morning. In the UK it is called:

- Concerta XL which works up to 12 hours
- Equasym XL which works up to 8 hours
- Medikinet XL which works up to 8 hours

Some children may need the medicine everyday while others need it for school days only.

The doctor may stop the medicine from time to time to see if the child still needs it.

While taking the medicine, some children may not eat well and at times do not sleep well. However, this gets better by changing the dose and / or the time of the medicine.

What is Atomoxetine?

Atomoxetine is another medicine which is taken as a capsule once or twice a day. It is a long-acting medicine and should be taken every day. It is also called Strattera in the UK.

The child starts improving within a few weeks of taking this medicine. It takes about 6 to 8 weeks for a lot of improvement to be seen.

Sometimes the child may feel a little sleepy and at times complain of a bit of tummy ache or headache, while taking this medicine. However, with time and changing the dose of medicine, the child generally feels better.

Do children grow out of ADHD?

The doctor said that many children get better after treatment. They can grow up to become happy and popular adults. However, some youngsters continue to have a few problems.

The doctor suggested that Tom could benefit by trying one of the medicines.

He also said that it is important to use the behavioural techniques both at home and at school.

Tom's parents wanted to try the medicine. Tom agreed and took the medicine every day.

Tom and his parents have also followed the helpful hints given by the doctor.

Tom tried hard to behave himself. He is better organised now. He tries to keep his bedroom nice and tidy. He is able to focus on tasks for much longer. As a reward, he chose to watch his favourite DVD.

After some time Tom's parents noticed that he was a lot better. He calmed down a lot. He is now able to sit still and do his homework. He has fewer tantrums.

Tom had lots of fun with his family when they went to France during the summer holidays. Tom's parents gave him Rover, the dog as a special birthday present.

His teacher says that Tom is now concentrating a lot more. He is not calling out or shouting in class as before.

He is behaving better. His schoolwork has also improved.

Mrs Bright.

Congratulations! Tom, you've done well in the test.

Tom says he now feels much better. He no longer gets into trouble in the playground. He is a popular boy at school with lots of friends.

Please turn over to the next page to meet Laura...

Here is the story of Laura which will tell you something more about ADHD in girls.

Laura is a 7 year old girl who lives with her parents in a town next to Tom's village. She is the only child in the family.

Laura's dad is a businessman and owns a small restaurant. He is a good friend of Tom's dad and they often meet at the local football matches. He got to know about Tom's ADHD and how well he was doing after the treatment.

As Laura was also having some problems, her parents went to see their family doctor. He referred Laura to a specialist centre – Dr Smart and her team.

Dr Smart

Laura's parents say that at home she can be very stubborn and often does not do as she is told. She is strong-willed and likes to be in control.

 She can be attention-seeking and very demanding at times. Sometimes she has temper tantrums. In a temper she gets into a bad mood and screams though she settles downs quickly. After a little while she says 'sorry'.

At home she is generally a quiet girl but finds it hard to concentrate and finish her homework. She often day-dreams. She is forgetful and tends to misplace her pencils and books.

Laura's parents say they love her very much as she can be a lovely girl who enjoys fun and in-door games. She also has a good sense of humour. At home, she likes reading and also playing with Fluffy, the cat.

The teacher says that Laura has a very short attention span in class. She has a lot of difficulty concentrating.

Miss Cheery

Laura is easily bored. She also day-dreams in class.

Laura is a little fidgety and makes careless mistakes in her school work. Her handwriting is untidy. She is not very organised and frequently loses things.

She is falling behind in her school work although she can do well with more concentration.

Laura is a lovely girl who is very polite and always tries to please others. She has lots of friends at school.

The doctor went through Laura's school reports and also the forms completed by Laura's parents.

Laura had a general health check-up and some tests to check her development. The doctor said that Laura was fit and healthy.

She then explained to Laura's parents that Laura has got ADD. Laura's parents have heard about ADHD but not ADD. They asked the doctor several questions.

 What is ADD?

The doctor said that ADD is the short name for Attention Deficit Disorder, which means Laura has ADHD without hyperactivity. It is also called Inattentive type of ADHD.

What does **'Inattention'** mean?

Because of Inattention, Laura has the following problems:

- Has trouble paying attention
- Has difficulty organising things
- Does not appear to listen
- Is forgetful and loses things
- Not able to follow instructions
- Is easily distracted
- Makes careless mistakes

What did the doctor advise?

As was suggested for Tom, the doctor recommended some behavioural techniques to be tried both at home and school. She also mentioned about a Parent Training Programme.

She talked about different medicines for ADHD and suggested Laura try one of the medicines.

Laura's parents attended the Parent Training Programme to understand and learn to manage Laura's behaviour. They are more confident now and are able to deal with Laura's problems at home.

Laura was happy to try the medicine to help her pay attention at school. She took the medicine during school days and skipped it during weekends and school holidays.

The teacher also helped Laura with some extra learning support and advice.

How is Laura doing at school?

After a few weeks, the teacher said that Laura improved, became less fidgety and more focused on her school work.

She was not day-dreaming in class any more. She made good progress with higher grades in literacy and numeracy.

Laura's parents are pleased that she is doing so well both at home and school.

They can reason with her when she gets angry. Laura rarely has tantrums now. She does her homework without too much fuss.

Laura invited many of her friends to her birthday party this summer. Tom and his sister Jenny also went along to the party. Laura had lots of presents. All the children had a fantastic time.

Parents can contact the doctor or nurse for further information about ADHD. In addition, the following sources may be helpful and are available through ADDISS.

Books for children

Zak has ADHD for 4 to 7 year old children by Jenny Leigh

My Brother's a World Class Pain
A sibling's guide to ADHD
by Michael Gordon

Books for parents

Understanding ADHD- A parent's guide to Attention Deficit Hyperactivity Disorder in children by Dr Christopher Green and Dr Kit Chee

1-2-3 Magic- Effective discipline for children 2-12 by Thomas W. Phelan